Chakana

Chakana

Poems by

Myra Tejada Rasmussen

© 2025 Myra Tejada Rasmussen. All rights reserved.
This material may not be reproduced in any form, published,
reprinted, recorded, performed, broadcast,
rewritten, or redistributed without
the explicit permission of Myra Tejada Rasmussen.
All such actions are strictly prohibited by law.

Cover design by Shay Culligan
Cover image by Catherine Chu on Unsplash
Author photo by Myra Rasmussen

ISBN: 978-1-63980-750-5
Library of Congress Control Number: 2025937991

Kelsay Books
502 South 1040 East, A-119
American Fork, Utah 84003
Kelsaybooks.com

for my daughter, Zealie
I love you mostest to the postest . . .

Acknowledgments

Thank you to the following publications, in which versions of these poems previously appeared:

Boundless 2025: The Anthology of the Rio Grande Valley International Poetry Festival: "Golden Length of Summer"
Home Planet News Issue 11: "Arroz con Leche," "Awana Kancha"

I'd like to thank all my creative writing professors, visiting writers, colleagues, and students who have taught me so much about the art and craft of the written word.

I would like to give a special thank you to Mark Cox, for the generous time and attention he has given to every one of my poems in this collection.

Thank you to Malena Mörling and Lavonne Adams who both taught me how essential it is to relay the truths, trials, and tribulations of the real world through a poetic lens.

Also, thank you to Christina Garcia for introducing me to Anne Carson's Autobiography of Red for which the idea of this collection was born and to A. Van Jordan for reminding me to take special care of the poems in this collection.

A very special thank-you to my parents, Carlos and Myra Tejada, for being my biggest fans, especially my dad for reading every one of my poems repeatedly and offering such beautiful insight. I wouldn't be a poet had it not been for him.

My biggest thank-you to my husband, Erik Rasmussen, for his unconditional love, support, and understanding. Erik, thank you for always believing in me and my writing.

And finally, thank you to my daughter Zealie, my biggest and brightest achievement.

Contents

Introduction 11

Prologue 13

Chakana 1 ~ Kay Pacha

Recognition 17
Night Mercado 19
Estofado de Pollo 22
Ode to Don Marco, El Gringo 23
Girl at a Rest Stop 26
A Winter's Day 28
Personal Conversations with Pablo Neruda: One 30

Chakana 2 ~ Ucu Pacha

Flor de Caña 35
Tia Hermelinda Invites Me for Tea to Tell Me About Her
   Husband's Passing and His Ghost 36
Personal Conversations with Pablo Neruda: Two 38
El Limón 40

Chakana 3 ~ Hana Pacha

When My World Smelled of Garlic 45
Golden Length of Summer 46
Personal Conversation with Pablo Neruda: Three* 47
Arroz con Leche 49
Night Flight 51
Awana Kancha 53

Epilogue 55

Introduction

Chakana is the Quechua name for the Inca Cross, a symbol that is known in other mythologies as the Tree of Life. It is one of the most enduring symbols of the Inca civilization.

At the heart of the symbol is a circular hole, which represents the city of Cusco, the capital of the Inca Empire and navel of the Incan world. Surrounding this circle are four planes representing Air, Fire, Earth, and Water. In its entirety, the 12 points of the cross represent realms, sacred animals, affirmations, and life points.

This collection is divided into 3 sections, each focusing on the realms and the sacred animals represented within each realm. They are: 1) *Kay Pacha,* the world of our everyday existence, represented by the puma 2) *Ucu Pacha,* the underworld inhabited by spirits of our ancestors, represented by the snake, and 3) *Hana Pacha,* the upper world inhabited by the gods, represented by the condor.

Also scattered throughout this collection are poems I have titled "Personal Conversations with Pablo Neruda", based on his poetry collection *The Book of Questions* (translated by William O'Daly), where I attempt to answer the questions that I found interesting and meaningful.

As a Peruvian/Mexican/American woman and poet, my goal for this collection is to introduce the reader to a culture that I am very proud to call my own. A culture filled with vibrant colors, smells, flavors, landscapes, language, and most importantly, the role of family in everyday life.

Prologue

The Daughter of Moon
1200 AD

Manco Capac rises from deep waters, his skin drips
gold. Lake Titicaca boils in his heat. Mama Ocllo rises, rips
a part of her moon rib; floats on it, extends her hand to Manco.
The water warms their bodies like alpaca blankets.
She is not his mother. She is his sister.

Where is the island? Manco asks. *Close
your eyes,* she says, guiding him
with her light of lilies, violets, sweet
vinegar. The water turns dark as mud. Then Sun.
Isla Del Sol, he whispers in her ear. She prefers moon.

The word 'moon' is endless so long as there is breath to give.
'Sun' off the tongue is quick and fleeting. Manco walks the island,
embosses a large footprint in rock. Mama Ocllo stays behind
in water. She has no footprints to give. Only shadows.

Mama Ocllo, leave the water and build us a fire
      But Manco, it is not cold and I am tired
But I cannot find my shadow
      Look harder
I need light
      You are light
Not anymore

Manco Capac flakes gold from his skin,
paints her forehead and cheeks with streaks
of his shimmer. *Let me,* Mama Ocllo says softly
then undresses him until only bones come
between him and her heart.

  Careful she says.
With your bones?
  No, with my heart.

He builds a sun temple with her bones,
on the northern edge of the island. The walls shine
even in dark, because he is gold and she is moonlight.
While Manco Capac sleeps, Mama Ocllo walks
to the water's edge, wades in
until lake water seeps into her womb,
until their son rises from deep waters
balancing boulders in his hands.

She names him *Sinchi Roca*. Magnificent warrior.
His first words are to become the language of their people.

Chakana 1 ~ Kay Pacha

The puma prowls
the Andes alone, never
needing to be seen. He explores
this earthen range with purpose, balance—
an enviable perseverance. Searching for refuge,
the puma lurks behind graying leaves of evergreens, awaits
acceptance, a beckoning home to that intimate feeling I find myself
  seeking.

Recognition

La Punta, Peru

It is not her eyes I recognize, black and heavy
like clumps of coal masking her despair,
her loneliness that keeps her up at nights.
There is a deepness within them, untraveled. A reflection,
perhaps of this one room cinder block home.
Rain seeps through the gaps of its thatched roof,
collects next to us in buckets for drinking water,
tomorrow's laundry, or for bathing her infant son.

Nor is it her hands that call to mind my own.
Hers, callused, cracked, stained
from the hard labor of *la chacra,* the monotony
of the constant digging into dirt for a better life.
Her hands begin to unclench as she tells me
about brief respites by the *higuera* tree,
how she escapes to that one moment; a time
when, upon devouring passion
fruit and figs under the shade of its branches,
juices dripped over and between
her fingers while her husband kissed the nape
of her neck. Then how the intimacy of their hands
traveled over contours of hips, bellies, thighs,
finally resting in palms, getting lost in them.
Knowing what she knows now, she confesses
she'd stop time the moment right before
her fingers intertwined with his and shape the words:
This is enough. Right here. Please, don't leave me.

Her feet hold the weight
of what she has carried
bundled together on her back—
potatoes, figs, fresh bread,
small jars of morning milk, her baby boy.
The burden of her husband's passing
seen in the peculiarities of her feet,
how the curves of her toes
claw at the earth with every step, how
each missing toenail must reveal a story.
There is rudeness in my wanting
to touch them, to wash them, to feel her
every bone and muscle in my hands.

It is her skin and only her skin
where I find recognition.
Our bronze skin sheltering us,
outlining our every beauty mark.
But how does it define us?
This is what I've come here to understand:
what becomes of the shadow when the sun sets?
And when I say, *please share with me
your stories,* her lips curve upward, force a smile.
She dips a ceramic cup into the bucket and hands it to me.
Rain continues to quietly drip. Her son nestles in,
begins to suck sweet milk from her breast.
She looks at him with such tenderness, as if to say,
The trick is knowing
      when the sun casts a shadow, it also makes it shimmer.

Night Mercado

La Paz, Bolivia

Crowds of Bolivianos descend
from the poverty of El Alto,
gather in the streets
of the night *mercado* in La Paz.

You become intoxicated
by the music of it all,
how the collage of their bodies
creates a controlled chaos,
a choreographed dance of legs
from booth to identical booth.
Vociferous men repeat
¿cuánto cuesta?, a bartering
for coca leaves, for one of thousands
of different light bulbs,
stiletto heels, red and green
striped tube socks, toilet seats, or
the most intimate of lingerie.

You can't seem to shake this clatter
of worn heels on cobblestones
drowned only by the clamor of car horns,
heads jutting out from battered minibus windows
arms flailing, men yelling, *¡muévete carajo!*

It's quite paralyzing here,
even the smells have sounds:
Eggs frying in oversized iron pots
for *silpancho,* the sizzling of sausages,
soft thuds from fresh rolls
dropping into barrels, the dripping
of fig jelly from empanadas, and
how the strawberry juice swishes
in plastic bags tied in knots.

You hear the maddening sounds of mutts
barking, large ones, small ones, always
in packs of three. Notice how they scurry
between people's legs, under tables,
sniffing at trash littering sidewalks,
stores, and streets. They challenge
homeless women for leftovers hidden
under wash buckets, for small pieces
of fried chicken still on the bones
in napkins next to sewage drains,
for fruit still attached to the peels, or
perhaps for a piece of melted chocolate.

A young boy, no older than 12,
pushes a wagon carrying a boom box,
the vibration of the bass awkward
inside of you. You notice a couple holding hands
walk by. When the man turns his head
towards the woman, sings along to the song
Hay tantas cosas que me gustan hoy de ti,

you blush. And when her exhilarating laugh
echoes in the valley, everything around you
becomes still and you recognize,
even among these crowds,
just how lonely you are.

It's sensible to suppose agony dominates
in all this suffocation. Yesterday you wondered:
How can people live like this? But tonight,
you begin to discover the beauty in this chaos, feel
the melody these sounds bring to you, how you want everything
about this place to change you. So, you ask:
How do their lives illuminate the night sky,
12,000 ft above anything I come close to calling home?

Estofado de Pollo

La Punta, Peru

I watch Tia Mery snatch the chicken, hoist it from the coop, then snap its neck with two flicks of her wrist. The bird spins, convulses, then dangles, limp in mid-air. At her kitchen stove, Tia Mery quips *como si nada* then dips the chicken into a pot of boiling water. Thick bubbles penetrate its pores. It gives one final thrash as Tia Mery pulls it from the pot and inspects its worth. She slaps it onto the floor over the front page of *El Comercio* then commences plucking until the chicken is naked, exposed, and ready for butchering. She hands me a cleaver from the counter, tilts her head in the direction of the chicken, and nods. I'm compelled to give a repulsive "whack" to the base of its neck, sever its head from its body. And in doing so, I know how later, I will sit with my family at the dinner table here in La Punta and listen to my father, after taking sips of her *estofado,* tell his brothers how impossible it is to find these flavors in the States. How he'll smile with great pride, saying it feels so good to be back, lift his beer, and give a resounding *¡Salud!* Their glasses will clink with mine as they respond *bienvenidos* while my father leans over to me, whispers, Tia Mery tells me you're a natural. I know all this as I pick up the chicken head from the floor, its steadfast blue gaze telling me that despite my efforts, I do not belong here.

Ode to Don Marco, El Gringo

Quime, Bolivia

Tonight, let's go down
to the traveling circus,
Don Marco,
mingle with the clowns.

Wear your flannel pajamas
with your ridiculous tie, the one
stitched with miniature golden
retrievers. Don't forget
the red, white, and blue
cardigan you save for "special
occasions" or the cheap bottles
of cabernet you've been drinking
with us and your visiting Polish friend.
While pouring me another glass, you said,
This family circus comes once every five
or so years. It's nothing big. But
it's something.

Last night, you told me of your exodus,
Don Marco,
your disdain for American politics
and the invention of the phone.
You shared with me how the peaceful,
hidden mountainside of Quime
named you, whispered
no one will find you here
nestled within transplanted
eucalyptus trees and vulnerable *tarucas*
feeding on your garden's white clover.
Always the dreamer,

you decided to build this hacienda
over the years with your arthritic hands,
brick by placid brick, until
your teeth began to fall,
becoming wedged in your long,
grey beard. And when your wife left you
with mounds of debt and dirty dishes
you said, *No matter.*
Home is not just a place, it's a feeling.

It rests in your kitchen
with its secret maple syrup recipes
and its concoctions of quinoa and bananas
mixed with your aphrodisiac potion.
It is in the first fleeting moment
you smell fresh bread baking
in the *tienda* down the street. How
the red tablecloth newly draped
over the stool outside the store means
come get it while its hot.
It's found during your arduous hikes
to the tops of these Andean mountains
where glacial blue lakes lay dormant.
It reveals itself at the peak,
when the red setting sun
invites you to shed all inhibitions
and frolic with celestial spirits.

So, later tonight,
as we walk down towards town,
while children run beside you
yelling your nickname,
El Gringo,
and crowds begin to huddle
by the makeshift circus tent
awaiting the flying trapeze,
please keep telling me,
Don Marco,
what Quime means to you,
so perhaps, one day,
it will mean the same to me.

Girl at a Rest Stop

Quime, Bolivia

A young girl immediately approaches as I get off the bus. She is tall, very skinny, wearing green pants she's outgrown, a faded pink hooded sweater, and black sandals made from used tires. Her hair is pulled back, wisps fall on her dusted cheeks, cover her eyes. She holds out her hand to me, asks ¿*Cinco bolivianos?*, less than it would cost to buy bottled water back home, but enough to feed her the *sopa de gallina* and *lomo saltado* advertised on the cardboard sign next door. Beside her, in a dirty white bucket, she passes out plastic baggies tied in knots filled with *jugo de fresa*. Not real strawberry juice, rather, dirty well-water colored with red dye, flavored with sugar. Around me, passengers poke small holes into them with straws, then close their eyes as they savor the sweet flavor in this cold mountain desert, a brief repose from the long bus ride. Having traveled in Bolivia for months, I know too well the uncertainty of the day-to-day: the planning and re-planning of remote routes, the budgeting for cheap meals, the acceptance of cold showers in shared bathrooms, and the luxury found in a quiet room. Exhausted, I look to her again as I walk away. But she persists, follows me with her bucket as I find a small bush to pee behind, follows me to the small *tienda* where I purchase salt-water crackers, even follows me back outside, all the while tugging at my coat, asking for money. I have witnessed this scene many times before. How every rest stop is filled with children asking for money, while their mothers crouch nearby breast-feeding or too crippled to walk. And these children all have eyes that are hungry, all have tattered clothes, all in need of a bath. This girl is no different. At least, that is what I tell myself as I board the bus again. She tugs at my jacket, this time with more force. I turn around, hear the desperation in her *señora por favor*. Reluctantly, I step off and give her *cinco bolivianos*. She extends the colored water, I tell her *no gracias,* but she forces it into my hand as I reboard, and as the bus drives away, she stands there with a smile, waving me goodbye. I rest my head against the bus seat, the baggie limp on my lap, and wonder if perhaps I can learn from her persistence. What would that be worth? Where would it take me?

A Winter's Day

Uspallata, Argentina

for Erik

My love, I won't remember that winter's day
for our walk down a desolate path
weaving through a desert, its unnamed valleys.
I won't call to mind those dog carcasses
swarmed by flies, or the discarded tire sandals
on the side of the road next to trash bags
ripped open by coyotes. No.

Instead, I'll remember it as the day you guided me
past that path to a secret place. *It's just a little
further up* you said, my restlessness beginning to show.
Upon reaching the clearing, a spectacle of big, beautiful
boulders decorated in pastels.
How the pinks glistened, the yellows
exhilarated, and you—
as you held my hand with such affection, I swear
I saw you blushing.

I'll recall how you had me sit perfectly still, perched
atop a lone boulder that seemed to exist
just for us. My sweat dripped and burrowed
between the cracks, while you,
standing below, said to me in a discernible whisper,
will you marry me for real?

I will never forget, how in that one instance,
vermillion reflected from our eyes
as we looked to the horizon, noticed how it burned
like a rich, tended fire with no particular flame.
And how, for the first time in my life,
after hearing *for real,* I finally understood
the feeling of an endless presence
and believed anything was possible.

Personal Conversations with Pablo Neruda: One*

*What is it that upsets the volcanoes
that spit fire, cold, and rage?*

*Do tears not yet spilled
wait in small lakes?*

*Or are they invisible rivers
that run towards sadness?*

                    A blaze of flowers,
                    an area rug soaked in
                    wine—undiscovered fires
                    waiting in my private corners
                    for him.

                    What will he find?
                    An archipelago of mischief?
                    Pastures of primroses?
                    Perhaps
                    untethered yellows
                    searching for a horizon,
                    the answers
                    to the thousand questions
                    that remain and on top
                    of them a thousand more.

                    When he's inside me,
                    how fulfilling it will feel
                    to finally cry
                    into the lake of myself,
                    to create cool waters for him
                    to swim towards,

to dive deeper
into our reflections while
white petals float above
towards a raging river.

*Neruda, Pablo. *The Book of Questions* Translated by William O'Daly. Copper Canyon Press, 1991. Page 8. Lines 1–2. Lines 6–9.

Chakana 2 ~ Ucu Pacha

The snake
burrows deep
deeper still
slithers
until no longer comfortable in its skin.   A shedding
of everything it knows, everything
it feels, then rawness of quieted small bones
telling it to start again
build from within
live
within new skin
that beautiful sheath of gold shielding all inhibitions.

Flor de Caña

Omotepe, Nicaragua

It's an unbearable heat in January. We welcome the hush
from one lone breaker as it overlaps our toes. Sugar cane
sweat pours out of us while you strip off your clothes,

inviting me to swim naked in Chaco Verde waters.
I concede, become swallowed by this blue lagoon within a lake
within an ocean, feeling once again jolted, this time

by an afternoon thunderstorm. The cool poignant
pricks of rain feel different on my skin and I find it refreshing,
soothed by the rhythm of these oscillating waves. You say, *I'm
 sorry,*

and I believe you. Or rather, I want to believe you,
tempered by the sight of your tanned back
curved like that aubergine omen

setting on the horizon. At least, I call it an omen when you say
Don't worry, the Flor de Caña will taste extra sweet tonight
just as the last bit of blue sky falls behind us.

Meanwhile, in the distance, Volcán Concepción is cloud cupped
while jealous winds ravage her ridgeline, a sign,
that in time, she will erupt again.

Tia Hermelinda Invites Me for Tea to Tell Me About Her Husband's Passing and His Ghost

Lima, Peru

Hierba luisa, mint, orange peels,
a mystery spice that lingers, leaves
simmering in the tiny kitchen
where she tells her story:

    ¡Fue muy directo!

Her husband asking for his ashes
to be spread in the Rimac River
so he could drift past La Punta, to the cold
Pacific waters then finally rest at the bottom of the earth.

Careful to respect this final wish,
Tia Hermelinda made her way to the riverbank
dressed in her Sunday best but then

    ¡Carajo! ¿Cómo es posible?

A drought in Lima had caused the river to shrivel
to a puddle, three tea pots worth of water.
She whispered,

    Te encuentro en mis sueños

then upended the urn, shivered
as ashes clung to her dress,
before wafting gently towards water
to become mud.

And now, Tia Hermelinda pours me
another cup of her tea,
sweetens it with anise, canela, then looks gingerly
out the window to see if his ghost will appear
as dusk approaches. She asks me,

    ¿Lo ves?

while she stirs her cup. After some silence,
she leans in to confess she had prayed
for that drought, for the river to turn to sand,
so her husband couldn't float away, then
adds with a smirk,

    Fue mi culpa,
    pero se queda conmigo

taking sips of her tea while
grinding his sand in her teeth.

Personal Conversations with Pablo Neruda: Two*

*In France, where does spring
get so many leaves?*

*Where can a blind man live
who is pursued by bees?*

*If the color yellow runs out
with what will we make bread?*

                                        As he left me, he asked
for the name of that town
in France—the one where
years ago, one spring,
we had found ourselves
noticing how each vine
delicately sprawled up
the white spine
of Eglise St Jean.
How later that night,
he would trace on my back
its leaves wrapping around
every curve and imperfection,
around anything
needing to be held.

And when his finger reached
the hollow of my neck, my
skin began dripping honey.
Bees
suddenly
swirled
around us

humming
what he hoped would become
a familiar tune.
Wings brushed
against that soft spot
behind my ear,
the one he'd find later
that night, kissing it gently,
the buzzing still in our ears,
our sheets sweat soaked.

If I could, I'd go back,
find bits of honeycomb
to preserve in a jar, label it
"marriage,"
use it later to knead bread
until the dough sweetens,
until I find myself
wrapped around those years
lost, listening for the
humming I once ignored.

---

*Neruda, Pablo. *The Book of Questions* Translated by William O'Daly. Copper Canyon Press, 1991. Page 2. Lines 3–8.

El Limón

Waterfall near Samaná
Dominican Republic

>We rode horses to El Limón. Brown horses,
mine named *Cacao,* or Chocolate. Yours
named something I cannot remember.
It had rained that afternoon
and smells of basil and mango mixed
with the rawness of the thick red mud.
Our guide, a poor, young girl,
walked between our horses,
kept a loose hold on *Cacao's* muzzle
while her rain boots sloshed with every difficult step.
Suddenly, it began to rain again. Hard.
She placed a used, white plastic bag over her head,
protecting her tight braids. She knew this weather,
knew in this rainforest, things could change instantly.
Along the path, she picked a pink grapefruit from a tree,
peeled it as she walked, offered us slices. You nodded
graciously, said *gracias,* then an unexpected *Wow! Honey,*
you gotta try this, while licking your fingers one by one.
The girl giggled, then looked to me,
noticed the uneaten slices held between my thumb
and fingers. Specks of dirt coated the fruit. Small gnats
rested atop its citrus seeds. As if understanding my hesitation,
a sadness filled her eyes,
an apologetic stare, believing she had nothing
better to give.
I recognized her offer then.
It was as if she was trying to say,
Welcome to El Limón. Release yourself
to these jungles, to everything unfamiliar and wild.
You were happy to finally see me concede, take a bite.

In that instant, grapefruit juices ran from my mouth, nestled
into the folds of me, into those familiar places
you traced effortlessly those nights before I fell
asleep. I remember how sweet citrus sugars mixed
with my body's salts, then the impulsive jump off
Cacao into the warm waters of the waterfall that
bellowed down and hard. How delicious it felt
discovering myself among her world of juices.
You became hypnotized by my transformation,
swam to me against the heavy waters, to tell
me *remember, THIS is who you really are.*
In the end though, your words were too heavy for me to carry
back, meant instead to stay beneath the waterfall,
sink slowly from the current's frothy foam
to that ledge of undercut rock, unreachable
by sunlight, breath, or our faith
in each other. I remember how, on the way back,
you rode with me on *Cacao*. It began to thunderstorm.
Bursts of lightning illuminated the wet green around us.
The young girl, knowing the path ahead would soon become
muddier, harder to traverse, told you to wrap your arms around me
tight. I should have asked her then *What should I do?*
Unlike me, she had something more yet to give.

Chakana 3 ~ Hana Pacha

The black condor
soars far above
the Andes mountains, his wingspan the length
of the Urubamba Valley.
He flies alone,
measures time
by the magnitude of his shadow,
measures distance
by the crisp updrafts
beckoning him
to time his wings to the rhythm
of my deep red longing for you.

When My World Smelled of Garlic

for Sara

Almond-shaped cloves of garlic,
the color of pearls, always
soaked in her old, iron pots filled
with *borracho* beans and Spanish rice.

I remember how her hands
always smelled of garlic, remember
her telling me how minced pieces
would dig under her nails and later
sprout delicate leaves while she slept.
How, in the morning, she would carefully
clip them, sprinkle bits over her tamales,
flour tortillas, and even
her famous buttered cookies.

She made my world smell of garlic and everything
about that smell was comforting and warm.

Today, her beans and rice no longer simmer,
her cloves have all been peeled and cooked,
there are no more delicate leaves
left for garnish. And too often, I find myself
so very empty. But whenever I smell the sweet
scent of garlic, I think of her and feel myself full.

Golden Length of Summer

During the golden length of summer, the kitchen curtains shine several shades of blue and this makes my mother fake-happy. She looks out the window for my father, fries eggs with extra butter. Wildberry preserves on the side. *Why is it called preserves?* I ask. *Because sugar keeps you sweet. Preserves your heart.* Then she kisses my forehead. The stench of burnt bacon from the blackened pan sizzles.

During the golden length of summer, my father toils the back-yard earth. In search of black soil. *Like tar* he says. *Needs to burn black as tar.* He stabs the hoe into the ground, small worms squirm to the top, suffocate in the air. I pick one up, watch it jiggle. Once, I saw my mother tear a worm in half. Both halves kept wiggling between her fingers, one more than the other. *Can it feel pain?* I asked. *No,* she said, as she dropped the pieces into her apron pocket. *Wouldn't it be nice to be a worm for a day? Bury yourself within quiet spaces of carrots? Swim in endless pools of heirloom tomatoes?*

During the golden length of summer, my mother learns to play with fire. The kind of fire that can leave skin scalloped. *I want to be cooked by love,* she says, then a match in her fingers and her world ablaze. *Does it hurt?* I ask her later while she lays on their bed covered in wet rose petals. *No,* she says as flakes of skin fall to the ground. Ants carry them away like sugar, back to the soil for my father to find.

Personal Conversation with Pablo Neruda: Three*

for Josephine

*And what did the rubies say
standing before the juice of pomegranates?*

*Who shouted with glee
when the color blue was born?*

*Why does the earth grieve
when the violets appear?*

                        Palm Sunday and a memory
                        of my mother cutting a lock
                        of her mother's hair,
                        my grandmother curled like a
                        sleeping child.
                        Mother touching her freckled
                        cheek one last time, feeling
                        just how soft Death feels.
                        Red fingernail polish—just
                        painted—begins to dry.
                        Grandmother's fingertips
                        remind me of rubies,
                        and my tears taste like
                        pomegranate juice,
                        small puddles collecting
                        at my feet.

                        I fight the impulse
                        to scream, to release
                        my sadness, taking comfort
                        knowing I whispered
                        I love you in her ear, watched

as her eyes flickered
one last time
with recognition
of everything that I am.

No. I don't scream.
Instead, I grieve in violets,
hues that mix well with what
grows inside me:
the knowledge
that I'm outliving those
I love the most
but don't know how to honor
this gift they've given me.

*Neruda, Pablo. *The Book of Questions* Translated by William O'Daly. Copper Canyon Press, 1991. Page 14. Lines 1–2. Lines 5–8.

Arroz con Leche

La Punta, Peru

for Daniel

The cow stands poised, ready. Udders sway,
tapping against the rim of the tin bucket.
My abuelito assumes his daily post on the stool,
and squats. His knees crackle and his bare feet
with those long toes, hug the ground while hands
alternate a rhythmic up-down, up-down, then—
release. Drops of cream begin to bounce and clink
like familiar notes from pan flutes. The bucket
slowly fills with warm milk, swirling in various
off-white shades. Abuelito continues milking
knowing the cow can give him more, knowing
it has to in order to pay last month's debts.

I watch curiously while barn smells
and colors filter through, find myself surrendering
to them, to the disgust of dirt and cow sweat and
human sweat and labor and bare feet and more
dirt again. Everything about this sentiment is
beautiful. How had I never noticed before,

brown, the color of abuelito's dry soil
waiting for rain? So much beauty
sleeping in the potential of it. Brown,
the color of untreated wood awaiting his attention,
perhaps gloss to make it shine.
Brown, the color of my own skin
during the coldest of evenings.
How beautiful it looks against light colors, how powerful
it feels against anything.
And brown, the color of cinnamon

sprinkled over the *arroz con leche* abuelita will cook
tonight, knowing it's my favorite. How the warm taste of sugar
and cinnamon on my tongue will mix with abuelito's words,
hijita, no recordamos los días. Recordamos los momentos.
Is there a color more delicious than that?

Night Flight

Monterrey, Mexico

for Edmund

Tacked to a hospital wall, a 25-cent poster of Jesus
frays at the edges. I sit
with four ladies at a waiting room table,
picking tea bags from a wicker basket,
pausing between sips to reflect.
What's happening is death.

Family continues to arrive throughout the afternoon,
mindlessly kissing each other hello on each cheek,
quickly catching up on societies' debutantes and
tabloid gossip in one long breath. How easy to forget
for a minute my mother's father dying in the next room
with so many tubes flowing from his body, the beeps
from machines comprising a symphony playing
Canto de despedida.

Passing time, wearing as many copper crosses
or medallions as necessary, we pray, recite Ave Marias
until the rosary beads feel heavy in our hands. We talk,
ask questions, share tabooed stories about affairs, divorces,
the time my great-grandfather abandoned his family
only to secretly start another one.

Ties that help us make sense of who we are,
or why I have a beauty mark under my right eye,
or why one day I could wake up and instead of making coffee,
decide to jump out a window, or why I once slept
with a married man and then bought ten new pairs of shoes.
From what I hear, my great-aunt once did too.

The hot water never runs out. The teas keep coming.
Peppermint, spiced-cider, chamomile, jasmine, juxtaposing
with the smell of cologne from my grandfather's room,
a smell more familiar to me than the man himself.

Sitting next to his bed one last time,
a desperate prayer transforms into a question,
Padre nuestro que estás en. . . . . el cielo?
but then I realize that's not the question
I really want to ask. Instead,

Does he know we know of his affair? Is he remorseful?
What did he say to my grandmother to make her forgive him?
And what does that forgiveness feel like?

But in the end, I kiss his forehead and can only say,
Goodbye,

then go home to Chicago on a night flight.
Looking out the window, I smell tea on my fingers.
I do not brush my teeth for fear the flavor will fade.
I think of family and the secrets
we choose to never share, and those that we do.
The identities we openly display, and those we keep close
from those closest. Then I think of my grandfather
and am overcome with a sadness in losing a man
I loved so very much but never really knew
and wonder what will become of me?

And then I don't anymore.
And then I do.

Awana Kancha

small llama farm near Pisac, Peru

for Mom

Crouched by looms made of llama bones,
women weave in synchrony, bodies swaying
to pan flute harmonies, around them bright yarn
twirling on drop spindles. My body is hypnotized by rhythm.

Recipes pass mother to daughter:
crush cochinilla bugs for red dye, add lemon
to blood for burnt orange, chisel from indigo rock
the marine blue buried in the deepest corner of sky.

Find bliss in the burgundies. Let smells of chocolate
and greens seep from nogal leaves,
rustle quietly through huarango trees.
And always, always set fire to the elements—

a fire that requires attention, an innate tenderness,
like the tenderness a mother gives her child,
a gift of sancha suncha violets wrapped in her words,
El tiempo todo lo cura. Mother, I think of you now

as an Incan woman offers me a scarf of the finest alpaca
sprinkled with bits of gold, as the crisp Andean air presses
against my face, while the black night uncurls its hands
over the mountain pass and releases me.

Epilogue

Manco's Footprint
Isla del Sol, Bolivia 2012

for Dad

We hike Isla Del Sol in a comforting silence.
Honeymooners wrapped in the whisk of late afternoon air, a crisp
breeze from Lake Titicaca, blends with the scuffling
of our footsteps. An occasional wave breaks
the deserted shore below.

>*It's like the air is singing*, you say
>>*What do you hear? I ask*
>*Listen closely. It's not me it's singing to.*

You take my hand, point to the Lake's horizon,
both blinding and tranquil. That time of day
when the sun reflects red, vermilion, then
bursts borealis blue at the surface.
We gaze at it for what seems like hours.
Finally, you break the silence,

>*Time to find that footprint.*
>>*But what if we can't find it? What if it was never there?*
>*Then you'll know.*

*

Comfort comes from recollections of my dad
reading Lorca, Bécquer, and Neruda during bedtime,
teaching me how beautiful Spanish sounds can feel
when they roll off the tongue, how important their melody is
to whom I'll become. Then stories
of the great Inca King, Manco Capac,
and his footprint embossed in rock
marking the beginnings of their history.

> *What's history, Daddy?*
> *The story of who we are,*
> *hijita, a collection of our*
> *memories.*

A collection I've built upon, memories of deliberate denials
trying to sooth hidden shame, temper the stigma
I believed being Peruvian carried
in this white, white world:
poor, dirty, an *other.*

But now, years later, not an *other,*
rather *Hispanic,* the word itself a syllabic song,
and my journey back, a search for reconciliation, a shedding.

> *Daddy, I'm so sorry. Read to me*
> *again. How does the story end?*

*

You are the first to find the footprint, a beautiful giant
press of earth. The mark of a man's weight made permanent.
I place my foot on top, watch how it becomes swallowed
by a presence greater than my own, the feeling of my dad
near, his comforting voice telling me:

> *This is who you are.*
> *Don't forget, love*
> *is born from mistakes.*

Quick my love! Take a picture! I tell you,
but instead, you walk towards me, kiss my cheek, whisper,
   Not just yet. Wait for the moment to find you and settle.

About the Author

Myra Tejada Rasmussen is an adjunct professor in the Creative Writing Department at the University of North Carolina-Wilmington (UNCW) where she teaches Poetry and Journal Writing. In 1999, Myra received her BA in English from the University of Notre Dame and in 2014 her MFA in poetry from UNCW. She has been a semi-finalist for the James Applewhite Poetry Prize and a finalist for the Poet's Billow Pangaea Poetry Prize. She lives in Wilmington, NC with her husband Erik and daughter Zealie. Myra loves the outdoors, running, traveling, cooking, and spending the summers in full adventure mode with her family in Colorado. *Chakana* is her first collection.

www.ingramcontent.com/pod-product-compliance
Lightning Source LLC
Chambersburg PA
CBHW031205160426
43193CB00008B/519